OrangeBooks Publication

Smriti Nagar, Bhilai, Chhattisgarh - 490020

Website: **www.orangebooks.in**

First Edition, 2021

ISBN: 978-93-92878-01-5

Printed in India

Of Seen And The Soul

Sarvesh Nikumbh

OrangeBooks Publication

www.orangebooks.in

"Dedicated To My
Wife, Kavita"

Preface

I am well aware that I was unable to introduce myself to the world as a poet in this age of technology. Life in this age is mostly associated with mobile devices, laptops, and so many electronic things that we use daily. These poems were meant to be shared electronically at first. I wrote around one hundred poems till now, which are mostly written in last three years. I was confused about publishing them, I had to think and rethink and rethink whether I should publish them online on social media platforms?

When I wrote them, my prime objective was to express myself lyrically. Those expressions in the poems were common life experiences, and the repeated feelings made me to show the spontaneous overflow of my feelings in tranquility.

In all this, my first preference is my job, I focused on my job first, writing is my hobby hence I write only after my professional commitments are fulfilled, it soothes me. After writing one hundred poems, I decided to share them on social media, but I was dissatisfied by it's reach. Hence in 2021, I decided to publish my first collection of poems by the title of "Sensible Senses: Songs of Soliloquy".

Now I am here with another collection of poems, each one of these poems contain my thoughts, which are near and dear to my heart.

I once read the lines by William Wordsworth in the preface of Lyrical Ballads, where he said,

"Several of my Friends are anxious for the success of these Poems from a belief, that, if the views with which they were composed were indeed realized, a class of Poetry would be produced, well adapted to interest mankind permanently…"

Acknowledgement

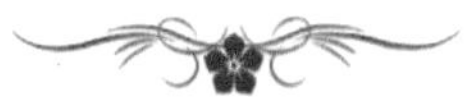

I can't forget the help and support that is always given to me by my parents. My brother is always by my side to support me in everything that I passionately do. To show my gratitude towards them, I have already dedicated my first collection to my mother, my father and my brother. This year one more person was added in the list, she is my wife. This book is dedicated to her.

I thank all of them who were a big help to me. My bank, in which I work as an employee, has supported me in publishing this work. I thank Bank of India to be with me always with my dream to become a writer.

Index

PART-1

Walking down the street,
I felt a need,
Tracking up my will,
I found the feed.

To speed my read,
To start my lead,
To write my poem,
To make my breed.

This deed to make a fortune,
Of words in books,
In literature of emotions,
In ponds with words as ducks.

Plurals I used often,
Where words demanded,
Singulars were sulking,
Being camouflaged as plurals.

As destination arrived,
A poem took shape,
Mind had it untied,
Heart tied it with hope.

Insufferable pains for the lied truths,
Intoxicated brains through the wild nights,
Insufficient patience in the matters of love,
Indulgent vibes from romantic talks,
Informative Texts in the bulky Books,
Indigenous relations with the native neighbours,
Is everything of these so unbearable,
That closeness in all these,
Or their validity true?
Hallucinations in all of them!

Seven suns;
each corner of the sky,
Except one;
reserved for the dark

Shameless;
not a nasty rhythm,
Fishes sing;
catch to see them

Waiting for people;
stood the mountain,
There it rose;
the joy in fountain!

Tricks played;
by this nature,
Above all;
Lies the truth of life.

Cradle in the dark woods,
Lying there hidden,
Sun won't shy it!
Embarrassed by the shadows!

Rusting away its beauties,
Robust veins of blood,
Dying with the air,
Bereft from the ocean!

The waves of burning desires,
In the sea of roaring blood,
The waves romance with thoughts,
Struggle to come out.

Shining in Sunshine,
Clouds also shimmer,
Blocking the path of light,
And bearing the weight of skies.

Run from one corner to the other,
Befriended by the wind,
So light they are,
Crowding earth everywhere.

At night they are scary,
Through the day they are beautiful,
When it rains; they seem sad,
In summer they seem happy.

Like balloons they float,
Carrying water above air,
Firing the same,
Gift greenery to us all.

Fighting among themselves,
throw lightnings anywhere,
While parting from each other,
Throw chilling water.

Soliloquy of thunder;
Either emotions of anger,
Or emotions of rage.

Soliloquy of wonder;
Either chatter of beauty,
Or chatter of joy.

Soliloquy of self;
Either thoughts of success,
Or thoughts of failure.

Soliloquy of sorrow;
Either failure in love,
Or failure in Life.

Soliloquy of success;
Either love for life,
Or love for the self.

Today I will not ask " how are you?"
But I will only say 'Happy Birthday to you!'
The world says, you are better than me,
I fear they are breaking the word 'We'.

I am jealous sometimes of your deed,
You know, why is that?
parents had us both, you in the lead,
you are older and I born late.

You are handsome and smart,
You have the charm, a beautiful heart,
Which fascinates the world,
Makes their blood cold.

May God bless you my dearest brother,
May God shower all kinds of joy,
Make proud our mother,
And like always you are a special boy.

Sullenly spoken words,
Spill out like;
They are worn out.

Suddenly broken hearts,
Sound like;
They are torn out.

Cameo of ragged moments,
Don't ask;
Before shattering the brains.

Dumb your life,
More you are safe;
Wicked creatures ignore.

Maybe everybody is wrong,
And only I am the one who is right,
Or I am the one who is wrong,
And everybody else is right.

Perception through fallacy,
Do I say it?
Illusion through truth,
Is it?

Grandeur in my life,
Stays in love that I get,
Fate decides my fortune,
That I hate!

I was sitting on that calm dark night,
Thinking about my past,
Someone touched me on my back,
I found no one there,
Again after some time,
When I sank down in my thoughts,
Someone touched my belly,
Again a fallacy of some kind,
I could not see anyone!
I Asked myself,
"Am I gone mad?"
Someone answered me,
"No you aren't,
I am your secret lover"
What could I say to that reply,
Then we talked with each other a lot,
Became so good friends that;
I never feel alone!

PART-2

Pain shackles the very existence,
Of Joy and Wonder,
Recollects all that has
For misery and sorry.

Tolerate what makes it so difficult,
Bubbling inside the heart,
Explosion of sadness,
Avoid this egoist monster.

Roaming inside brain,
Pain spreading damage,
Time wasted folly,
Release it from cage

Render your joy,
Crossing egoist obsession,
Age is not a toy,
Life is an Association!

Preference of staying put,
To keep my head low,
The ambitions are high,
And all this for what?

Preferences made quietly,
They aren't made to shut,
World hate your priorities,
They will ignore your things!

What you lose they won't gain,
They will win from your loss,
Your pulse to stop,
Is what they dream of!

Make yourself so strong,
Whatever flutters your heart,
Tell them to scare more,
For the beast in you to grow!

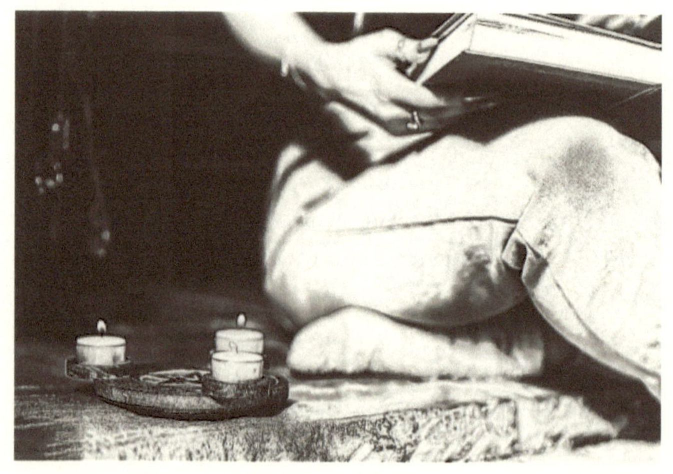

Devils burn in fire,
For the foolish sins,
Gods shine in light,
Brighter than moon.

Devils kneel before Gods,
Without any feelings,
Gods treat them all,
With sympathy to feel.

Devils have no shame,
They wander and beg,
Gods have the proud
Without anger and rage

Devils nested always,
Around the bad and sad,
Gods cure illness,
Make everyone happy and glad.

Avail me of grief,
For blaming my beloved,
For not caring much
Abandoning me her touch.

Tell me the truth,
Of her sorrowful agony,
With her love,
She did not hurt me

Fail me in love,
I am not worthy of it,
Still she is happy,
And I am morose!

Kill me for her joy,
Make me immortal,
I had to avail her for me,
Her love is eternal

Sarvesh Nikumbh

Life is testing me sometimes
I think; it voids me of space,
Then reminds me of Self,
And then Walks me into darkness

Life plays with my mind sometimes
I know; it shakes my soul,
Till I get back in my dreams,
And then wakes me up to horror

Life fails my ego sometimes,
It prays; it lifts my heart,
Keeping my secrets untold,
Still proud of my kind anger!

The moon shines bright,
When stars invade the skies,
Animals calming at night,
Wolves howling with cries.

Moon assumes the shape of bulb,
Sun jealous of his light!
Throught the windows,
Moon lits the rooms with delight!

Someone's uncle, someone's Treasurer,
Masses praise him,
Seems far but he is nearer,
Earths longlasting companion.

Classically described in romatics,
We sing his songs,
Closest to our eyes,
And closest to our heart.

17

If you say,
That I may,
Finish to crave,
Till I have my stay;
I obey:
Unless I try,
That I imply,
I prey to sink
Into the wall of clay,
Burst into the clouds,
Of shame and dismay,
Lie, which is far,
Far awa

I shut my door
Closed my eyes
On the weary roads
Rode without lies
not destination fixed
Yet feelings mixed
Its a dawn time,
May be greatly divine,
Season of grapes
Comes with winter breeze
Still some dark outside
To discover self, chances are wide,
Hell its fiery,
Feels looking at the rising sun,
Not yet fully burnt,
Still makes eyes blunt
I walked and waled for an hour now,
I didn't notice where I was going,
Coz i have devoted this day,
To meet the spiritual say!

Now the pollution started to rise
While the mob of vehicles rose,
I am here writing their prose
Tired and thirsty, I took a break,
Under a banyan tree by the side,
Sat their with sweat all over me
My shirt wet but still felt so nice,
As if i was tasting sugar all over my body,
I rested my spine with the spine of the tree,
Then took some water that was lukewarm,
Drank some sips, another heavenly feeling,
Then my handkerchief wiped it over the face,
It soaked all of the dust eaten sweat,
I thought i would be pale,
No i felt as if hearing a nightingale,
Still the rest of the day ahead,
Even bigger curiosity stayed

Frail skins damage a lot,
Frail minds fear a lot,
Bright lights hurt frail eyes,
clouds crowd in the frail skies.

The more fragile we are,
More the predators,
The more we are preyed upon,
The more they will haunt.

Stand alone or stand to fight,
Stand to correct the mistakes
Stand to be firm, make it right,
Pay the price, thats what it takes!

20

While swimming, I felt;
Like something was poking me,
I saw blood come out,
From my waist.

The blood came from,
The inner parts of Sorrow,
Every cut, every wound,
That gave me pain.

A painless body afterall,
Left its worries in that lake,
Water stole my mass
And I floated awake!

After a period of time,
I was totally weightless,
I could walk on that water,
Without any braces.

PART-3

A rainbow with bold colours,
never appears in the sky,
Its colours are washed away,
With the falling rain water.

A beautiful face of a bride,
Leaves all her desires,
When she leaves her home,
Starting a new life with husband.

An abstract painting,
Isn't that meaningful,
When it is owned by someone,
Other than it's artist.

A loveliest rose loses,
All its elegant charm,
When it is touched upon,
The stem where thorns are grown.

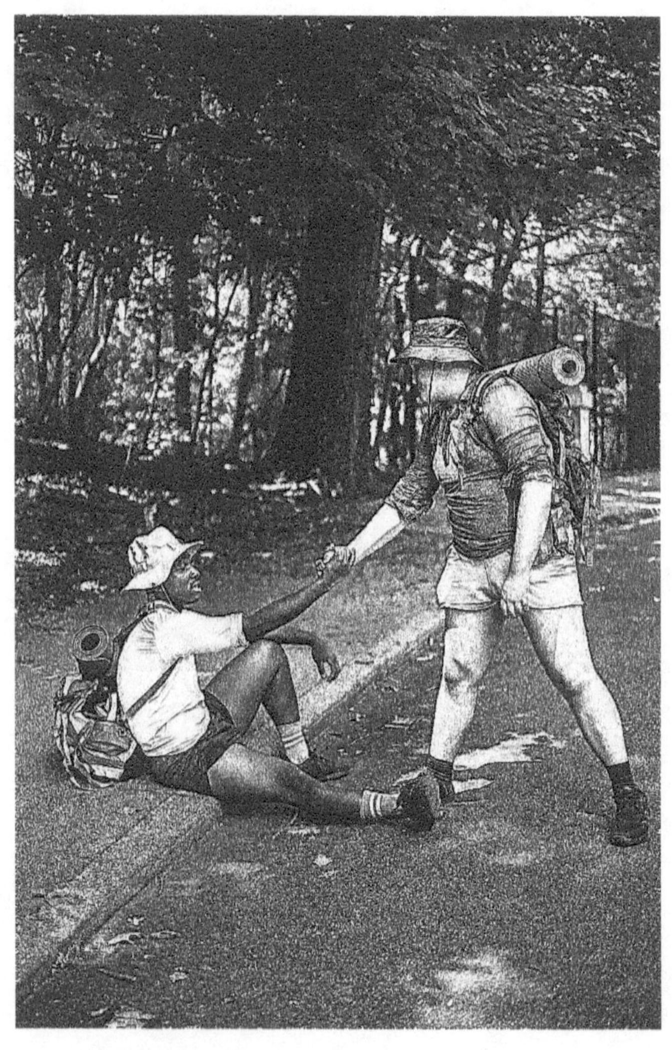

Walk bearing light in the eyes,
When walking through the dark,
Walk bearing warmth in the chest,
When walking through snow.

Walk bearing torch in your hands,
When walking through the caves,
Walk bearing kind heart,
While walking through beggar street.

Walk bearing rage in your hands,
When walking towards the aim,
Walk bearing strength in mind,
When walking through the horror

Walk bearing style in your swag,
When walking through riches,
Walk bearing simplicity in the body,
When walking through the real.

A Golden egg, carrying inside,
Some helpless creature,
Caught in a small egg,
Do they know it is there?

Ignorance to the egg,
Bliss to those who had its glimpse,
Why it is heavenly?
Golden, hence it is so!

Silly the nature of man,
Illusioned by this antic,
Touched by the naive feelings,
And greed for its collection.

When the autumn leaves fall,
But I wonder they lift our souls,
Then they carry the moods,
On their light breezes.

The touch of the fragrance from,
The wild wakening of souls,
From a deep sleep in,
Needless nights of sorrow.

The leaves then whisper to our
Heart beating boldly,
Bending the veins like,
Some snake in the fight.

Sing me a song,
Not of the ding-dong,
Or sing me a poem,
Must be small not long.

Am I so wrong?
That I need a song,
And you are tired,
Or are you stung?

Read me story,
Or read me a poem,
There is no hurry,
And nothing is lame

Just do something,
As I am bored,
Do as you like,
Nothing on blackboard.

Once it happened,
The dogs were barking,
At a squirrel in the bushes,
She looked odd.

She looked nice though,
She got scared of them all,
She had two heads
And she was about to fall!

The dogs barked louder,
They had a rhythmic echo,
Whole neighbourhood was shocked,
She was confused where to go.

Some tine passed like that,
Nature disfigured her like that,
People came to know that,
They pelted stones at them.

Always it happens so,
The weakest is barked at in fear,
She was shaking from head to toe,
The lonely little squirrel mere.

Rowing though small river,
I found a fish swimming,
She was taking leaps with me,
She was a dancing kind.

Lyrically danced side by side,
She took a rhythm of tide,
It was an unexpected ride,
Abd the river not so wide!

The shore too beautiful,
But less than her shine,
My boat was very dull,
The lovely fish was fine.

My home was very far,
The fish stopped somewhere,
In the way, I forgot all about her,
Maybe she stopped somewhere.

Once I was smiled at,
By an old lady,
She had some real theory,
She was the sorcerer.

Her mind with something crazy,
Would stare at me,
Her eyes like something hazy,
Would pair with me.

Did she bless me?
Or did hurt me the least?
What she had in her mind?
Or she was a beast?

Silhouette of mystery,
Wander though the lanes,
Here and there it dares,
It bears the fears!

The mystery of ghost,
A mystery so delusional,
An unsolved puzzle,
Who cares to involve?

Mistress hidden, or
Some Child unhappy,
Born it where no clue,
Husband killed by his woman?

Yes, it is a question?
Call a priest,
Or call an exorcist,
But save the nights to come!

A kind of portion is it?
Or any kind of food?
Which will take me there,
To that place, where peace
For my soul is present.

If no portion, a fruit,
Of some kind? To lift,
Me and my virtues,
Maybe it isn't a place,
It is hidden somewhere!

Take me there, my body,
Is waiting to stay there,
To relief my anguish,
On myself, and to have me,
To have that endless Joy!

www.ingramcontent.com/pod-product-compliance
Lightning Source LLC
LaVergne TN
LVHW091620170726
843492LV00007B/2529